Also by Charmas B. Lee and Janice K. Lee

The Power of Impact

Think, Say, Do – Becoming a High-Performance Christian

Think, Say, Do – Disrupting Systemic Cycles of Faulty Thinking

Resisting Success, the Battle Against Inertia

Stay In Your Lane

Run Your Race

A Different Kind of Champion

Hiding in Plain Sight

IT'S NOT BUSINESS, IT'S PERSONAL

Improving Workplace Productivity
Through COMMUNICATION,
CONNECTION AND
CONTRIBUTION

Praise for...

IT'S NOT BUSINESS, IT'S PERSONAL

"Charmas takes decades of experience and provides a concise, insightful exploration into the current landscape of our world, particularly focusing on the challenges faced in the workforce and the necessary shifts in leadership paradigms. As an expert writer, I am genuinely impressed by his depth of analysis and practical guidance.

In today's "debilitating discouragement" times, Charmas emerges as a beacon of hope and wisdom by astutely observing the struggles faced by individuals and organizations alike. He addresses the pervasive issues of burnout, apathy, and a diminishing work ethic. However, he offers a roadmap for personal and professional growth, emphasizing the critical role of leadership in shaping a brighter future.

One of the most compelling aspects of this book is its emphasis on the transformative power of self-awareness and personal mastery. By encouraging readers to embark on a journey of self-discovery, Charmas redefines the paradigm and lays the foundation for profound change and resilience in the face of adversity. What truly sets Charmas apart is his pragmatic approach to leadership development. By providing practical tools such as the "Attributes Scorecard" and anecdotes from real-life experiences, he empowers readers to assess their strengths and areas for improvement.

As an experienced leader and strong advocate of personal development, I wholeheartedly endorse IT'S NOT BUSINESS, IT'S PERSONAL as a valuable resource for anyone seeking to navigate today's complex and ever-changing world. Its blend of insightful analysis, practical advice, and inspiring anecdotes makes it a must-read for leaders at all levels. I commend Charmas for his dedication to empowering others and shaping a brighter future for individuals and organizations alike."

Chip Frazer, *Leadership Expert, Community Advocate, Defense Contractor, Lieutenant Colonel (Retired) US Army*

"Charmas and Janice Lee have written a tapestry masterpiece on developing high-performance employees. This book offers a broad and deep range of perspectives that will ignite change and impactful action for any leader seeking to move past the status quo traditional methods of obtaining and keeping high-performance thinkers and innovators and also becoming a high-performing leader.

Charmas and Janice Lee bridge the gap between theory and practice. This book introduces and expands on the model of embracing courageous self-evaluation, which makes this book not just a reading primer but rather a professional manual of durability, expectation, creativity and mental stamina.

This is a must-read book which will be a game changer for anyone wanting to embark upon the pursuit of personal growth. Read this book - and learn from two of the best in the industry. This is a tour de force in leadership and professional development. It's rare that a book can both captivate and enlighten its readers so profoundly, but this one does."

Dr. MelindaJoy Mingo, *Author: The Color of Cultures - The Beauty of Diverse Friendships, International Business Coach and Professor*

"Charmas Lee has done it again! Through his latest book, IT'S NOT BUSINESS, IT'S PERSONAL, he provides us with an insightful view of how we can lead our teams to be highly motivated and productive-or how we can fail to do so. I love how Charmas shares insights from other great authors and experts to complement his own expertise and perspective. Charmas shares his own personal experiences through his engaging storytelling, creating a wonderfully entertaining recipe for current leaders or any individual who wants to be their best in life for others. Clearly, it's not about business or ourselves, it's about the people. Well done, Charmas Lee!"

Ramon Alvarez, President & CEO, Alvarez Enterprises, Inc., Entrepreneur, Retired Corporate Executive, Small Business Owner, and Community Leader

"IT'S NOT BUSINESS, IT'S PERSONAL is not just a book title, it's a philosophy that resonates deeply in today's ever-evolving workplace landscape. It is insightful and delves into the core elements that drive productivity: communication, connection, and contribution. With a clear premise: traditional leadership styles no longer suffice. In this era, leadership is about influence and coaching. But before leading others, one must lead oneself, a journey of personal mastery and growth.

IT'S NOT BUSINESS, IT'S PERSONAL is a reminder that personal development isn't just about individual growth; it's the bedrock upon which trusting relationships and cohesive organizations are built. You're left with a roadmap to not just surviving but thriving in today's workplace."

Joe Aldaz, *President & CEO, Colorado Springs Hispanic Chamber, Lieutenant Colonel (Retired) US Air Force*

"I have witnessed firsthand the transformational impact that the right leadership approach can have on a workforce, especially in these challenging times post-pandemic. In this text Charmas focuses on personal mastery, emotional intelligence, and a paradigm shift in leadership which can make a remarkable change in company culture and employee engagement. If your team is riddled with apathy and burnout, this book will help you to create a thriving environment, resulting in increased productivity, creativity, and a renewed sense of loyalty. It's clear that by investing in our leaders and emphasizing the human element of our interactions, we're not just enhancing our work environment but also setting a new standard for success in nearly every industry. Charmas' insights into the transformational power of effective leadership and personal development are both profound and practical. Don't hesitate to read and apply this information, it could be the catalyst to phenomenal growth personally and professionally."

Bryan Aspenson, *CEO Amplified Advertising*

"Charmas and Janice Lee's book initially got under my skin because I was proud of telling clients, "it's not personal, it's business", as a way to separate their emotions from the process. Now they have challenged my assumptions and long held communicative direction by asking me to review a book entitled IT'S NOT BUSINESS, IT'S PERSONAL. And I have had to reevaluate my entire mindset and why I was putting into the world my long-held message.

And you know what, they are right! By using well-placed thoughts from some of my heroes in leadership and business, they have gently shown me the error of my ways. From my all-time favorite mentor, John Maxwell, and many other giants of leadership and personal development to bolster their premise, Charmas and Janice have masterfully made their case. With the addition of case studies and "The 10 Human Drives," they blew away many of my long-held assumptions about this space. The Table of Contents alone will give you a glance of the ride you are about to embark on. With topics like "Communication", "Advanced Personal Communication", and "Understanding Human Behavior" to name a few you can easily tell this dynamic team has thought long and hard about the subject at hand.

I am biased because I love Charmas and Janice, but ladies and gentlemen, I don't know of two individuals better suited to take us on this journey. One of the hallmarks of human behavior is having the humility to accept the possibility of being proven wrong and being open to new and enlightened information. I am so encouraged by this "new" point of view, and I believe you will, like me, applaud the fact that IT'S NOT BUSINESS, IT'S PERSONAL."

Frank Sinclair, *Chief Encouragement Officer, Dream Again, LLC, Author of Dream Again–Lessons on Leveraging Your Pain, Your Personal Life Coach and Your Personal Business Coach. Host and Founder of the International Vodcast, "Be Encouraged with Frank and Lisa".*

"Charmas and Janice Lee are outstanding coaches and more importantly they are wonderful human beings. Their motivation is not driven by financial currency, but instead is centered on human currency and their payday has turned others into champions in life. This book's message on workplace productivity is important and needed for the post COVID world. The message in the first few pages of the introduction, entitled Help Wanted, speaks to real world challenges for businesses leaders. The world is burning out and this book provides inspiration to change course. This book provides relevant lessons to change your life for the better."

Russ Council, *Business owner/Christ follower*

IT'S NOT BUSINESS, IT'S PERSONAL

Improving Workplace Productivity
Through COMMUNICATION,
CONNECTION AND CONTRIBUTION

Charmas B. Lee and Janice K. Lee

Military Might Publishing

Cover Design by Geraldine Villanueva, aka GV Designs and Team Lee

Military Might Publishing – www.militarymightpublishing.com

Publisher's Cataloging-in-Publication Data
Names: Lee, Charmas B., 1961- , author. | Lee, Janice K., 1965- , author.
Title: It's not business, it's personal : improving workplace productivity through communication, connection and contribution / Charmas B. Lee and Janice K. Lee.
Description: Colorado Springs, CO : Military Might Publishing, 2024.| Includes bibliographic references. | Includes 3 b&w illustrations. | Summary: Today's workforce desires a personal connection. This book offers a roadmap for personal and professional growth, emphasizing the critical role of leadership in shaping the future.
Identifiers: LCCN 2024912884| ISBN 9781961019065 (pbk.) | ISBN 9781961019089 (ebook)
Subjects: LCSH: Leadership. | Personnel management. | Employee motivation. | Organizational behavior. | BISAC: BUSINESS& ECONOMICS / Workplace Culture. |BUSINESS& ECONOMICS / Human Resources & Personnel Management. | BUSINESS &ECONOMICS / Business Communication / General.
Classification:LCC HF5549.5.M63 L44 2024 | DDC 658.3 L--dc23
LC record available at https://lccn.loc.gov/2024912884

Printed in the United States of America

Contents

Foreword   XVII

Introduction   XXI

    Help Wanted   XXI

    Attitude reflects leadership   XXV

    How do you measure up?   XXIX

1. Communication   1

2. Advanced Personal Communication (APC)   5

3. Understanding Human Behavior   9

4. Emotional Intelligence   13

5. Optimism   19

6. Connection   23

7. Contribution   27

8. Coaching   31

9. Change   41

10. Stress and Burnout   53

References   61

Acknowledgements   63

About the Authors   65

Foreword

To know Charmas Lee is to learn, understand and embrace winning! Charmas is about teaching athletes how to win, students how to excel in the classroom and leaders how to be successful in organizations and in life! Charmas is a genius, who is practical. I will explain later.

Charmas Lee is an elite, high-performance coach, professional speaker, author, sports and fitness professional. He is also a Certified Registered Exercise Physiologist, Certified Strength and Conditioning Specialist, and a Certified Level 3 USA Track and Field Coach, qualified to coach athletes at the Olympic level. As impressive as all of his well-earned credentials are, most significant is that Charmas is my friend.

My first encounter with Charmas was as a parent. In the off-season of my youngest daughter's sophomore year in high school, Charmas coached Andrea to prepare her to be a successful 400-meter runner. She qualified for the Colorado High School Track State

Championships. It was amazing watching Charmas train high school athletes to become scientists by understanding their bodies so that they could maximize their physical and mental abilities. Many of his athletes went on to win track scholarships in college.

Charmas has a presence that demands respect. He demands the best out of his clients, whether they are professionals or amateurs. They all seemed intimidated by him. Me too! I was so glad that he never commanded me to run. I am sure I would have! Maybe the most impressive thing that I've seen Charmas do was to take his immense knowledge of coaching athletes into the classroom to help at-risk students. Those same principles resulted in success with students earning academic scholarships to college.

Now, Charmas and Janice, his wife, have written, IT'S NOT BUSINESS, IT'S PERSONAL: Improving Workplace Productivity Through COMMUNICATION, CONNECTION AND CONTRIBUTION. It is a counter-cultural and business blueprint for success in corporate America, Charmas' next challenge for himself.

His genius is found in his counter-cultural approach to business, in which so many have echoed, "It's just business, nothing personal." However, we all know business can be extrmely personal when an employee feels his/her manager, supervisor or person in leadership above him or her doesn't listen to them or injustice is experienced for various reasons. This can not only lead to less productivity, but low moral or even termination. The introduction to this book is worth the price of it! Charmas assesses today's business climate and how to navigate it. We must check our attitude, which is critical to winning at work and in every other area of life. And so true to Charmas, he provides a self-evaluation opportunity in the introduction to help us know why we are where we are, where we go from where we are, and how to get there. This is priceless! Success in sports, work and relationships always requires putting in the work. The remainder of Charmas' and Janice's book explains the essential principles of communication and understanding human behavior (including ourselves). They also make us aware of emotional intelligence by defining it and how to apply this knowledge.

Next, Charmas and Janice help us to understand how optimism and pessimism impact us as individuals and organizational morale. Additionally, this book provides a road map to connection and contribution. Charmas and Janice give lessons and examples of how to coach effectively. They also address change and reveal the percentage-based research which shares how your organization will respond to change and why.

Possibly, one of the greatest gifts of this book is to guide us as individuals and leaders in an assessment to evaluate those in leadership or direct reports are in stress and burnout and how to restore emotional balance. If you want to or want your employees to say internally and outside of the office, that this is "the best job they have ever had" or "you are the best leader they have ever had," then reading IT'S NOT BUSINESS, IT'S PERSONAL: Improving Workplace Productivity Through COMMUNICATION, CONNECTION AND CONTRIBUTION is NOT optional for you.

Why am I so pro-Charmas? I have seen him in action. I have heard his praises sung by high school athletes, by their parents, by a district superintendent and by business leaders. If you read this book, you will join the choir in singing his praises because, remember, Charmas and Janice are about winning results.

Dr. Clarence Shuler, *President/CEO of BLR: Building Lasting Relationships, Chairman of the Board of the Fatherhood Co-Mission, Author of ten books, Diversity Consultant & Trainer, Co-author and Co-Speaker with Dr. Gary Chapman, New York Times Bestselling Author of The Five Love Languages of two books and former Sheriff's Chaplain*

Introduction

Help Wanted

It is no secret that our world has been and continues to go through a turbulent time of change. The landscape is lit with 'Help Wanted' signs everywhere you go. One of the post-pandemic realities is that many have lost their sense of self and are experiencing what I have coined to be a 'debilitating discouragement.' It affects every dimension of their lives, resulting in hopelessness, burnout, apathy, misdirected focus, and negativity, which in many cases has resulted in a less desirable work ethic.

Companies are desperate for capable and reliable employees. In many cases, entry-level starting wages have doubled, yet many employers have expressed concerns about employee loyalty. There are too many jobs and not enough people willing to fill them. Millennials now make up the largest sector of the workforce. According to the Gallop organization, 51% of people currently employed are looking for another job.

A long-time friend and colleague shared with me just five years ago that he believed he was in the greatest profession in the world and absolutely loved his work. In March 2023, I accompanied him to the human resource office, where he stated he was *"tired of doing the impossible for the ungrateful"* and turned in his letter of resignation.

The old leadership styles are no longer a viable solution, yet there must be a sense of greater expectations. If you want to achieve unparalleled levels of success, maintain the loyalty of your employees, or attract new ones, it will require a paradigm shift. According to John Maxwell, *"Leadership is influence, nothing more, nothing less."* The best leaders are the greatest coaches, and high-performance coaches have known for years that people are influenced not so much by logic but by emotion.

Before you can lead others, you must first learn to lead yourself. This will require personal mastery, which can be described as the ability to master your thoughts, behaviors, and actions. John Maxwell suggests, 'The first order of things to be changed is me, the leader. After I consider how hard it is to change myself, then I will understand the challenge of trying to change others. This is the ultimate test of leadership.

With your permission, I would like to:

- Take you on a journey of self-discovery

- Warm up your imagination

- Improve your personal and professional prowess

This is truly about personal development. Personal development may be described as 'the conscious pursuit of personal growth by expanding self-awareness, knowledge and improving personal skills.' According to Dr. Henry Cloud, author of Boundaries for Leaders, *"Personal development precedes the building of trusting relationships, and trusting relationships are an absolute prerequisite to developing an organization characterized by teamwork, cooperation, and contribution to the wider community."*

Attitude reflects leadership

There is a wonderful scene in the movie Remember the Titans where the football team's star defensive end, Julius Campbell, calls out team captain Gerry Bertier's lack of leadership of the recently integrated football team. Campbell shares his frustration regarding the lack of team cohesiveness and favoritism amongst the players. Team captain Gerry Bertier communicates his observations regarding Campbell's lack of character and negative attitude. A disgruntled Campbell retorts, *"Attitude reflects leadership, Captain."* While this movie is about American high school football, the sentiment remains: a good or bad attitude comes from the top down. Charles Swindoll is a former marine, pastor, author, and educator. He has written more than 70 books. Swindoll developed a quote that truly shares the power of attitude.

"The longer I live, the more I realize the impact of **attitude** *on life.* **Attitude***, to me, is more important than facts. It is more important than the past, than education, than money, than circumstances, than failures, than successes, than what other people think or say or do. It is more important than appearance, giftedness, or skill. It will make or break a company...a church.....a home.*

*The remarkable thing is that we have a choice every day regarding the **attitude** we will embrace for that day. We cannot change our past. We cannot change the fact that people will act a certain way. We cannot change the inevitable. The only thing we can do is play on the one string we have, and that is our **attitude**...I am convinced life is 10% what happens to me and 90% how I react to it. And so it is with you...we are in charge of our **attitudes**."*
~ Charles Swindoll

When we apply the numerical value to the alphabet, it shines a spotlight on some of the attributes of leaders and reinforces Mr. Swindoll's quote.

Knowledge, which has a numerical value of 96%, is a fundamental foundation for success. It provides the wisdom and understanding to make informed decisions and navigate life's challenges.

With a numerical value of 98%, hard work reflects the immense effort and dedication required to turn knowledge into tangible achievements. It reminds us that success rarely comes without diligent labor and determination. Hard work is the bridge that connects knowledge to accomplishment.

Attitude sets the standard with a perfect numerical value of 100%. It exemplifies the unwavering belief in oneself, the positive outlook that fuels perseverance, and the resilience to overcome setbacks. Attitude is the catalyst that transforms knowledge and hard work into genuine success.

A	1	N	14	K	11	H	8	A	1
B	2	O	15	N	14	A	1	T	20
C	3	P	16	O	15	R	18	T	20
D	4	Q	17	W	23	D	4	I	9
E	5	R	18	L	12	W	23	T	20
F	6	S	19	E	5	O	15	U	21
G	7	T	20	D	4	R	18	D	4
H	8	U	21	G	7	K	11	E	5
I	9	V	22	E	5		98%		100%
J	10	W	23		96%				
K	11	X	24						
L	12	Y	25						
M	13	Z	26						

Respect

Demonstrating respect does not just benefit you; it benefits everyone around you. No leadership behavior has a more significant impact on employee commitment and engagement, which is why the greatest leaders share this immovable respect for their employees. A study of nearly 20,000 employees around the world, conducted by Harvard Business Review in conjunction with Tony Schwartz, confirmed that respect had the most significant effect on employees—even more important than recognition, appreciation, communicating the vision, and providing feedback. Respect is rated even higher than opportunities for learning, growth, and development. Employees who feel respected are 55 percent more engaged. They also report 56 percent better health and well-being. Eighty-nine percent report greater job enjoyment and satisfaction, and 92 percent report increased focus and prioritization. Those who feel respected by their leaders are more likely to stay with the organization than those who believe respect is lacking.

How do you measure up?

C ommitment, dedication, and a good work ethic are the entry-level attributes of leaders who have achieved marginal levels of success. However, those who desire unparalleled levels of success look a little further and dig a little deeper. Please look at the descriptive and score yourself by circling a number next to each attribute. A perfect score is 45. A score of 35 or below suggests there is a need for improvement. After totaling your Score, identify the areas you would like to focus on to improve your overall Score.

1 = Poor   2 = Fair   3 = Average   4 = Good   5 = Great

Attribute	Score
Attitude: Is your general outlook or mindset positive? Are you typically pleasant, uplifting and optimistic and is it expressed by your external behavior?	1 2 3 4 5
Respect: Do you treat others with consideration, esteem and high regard?	1 2 3 4 5
Vision: Do you have a 4K High Definition clearly constructed vision for your organization?	1 2 3 4 5
Self-Motivated: Are you intrinsically motivated to accomplish your goals?	1 2 3 4 5
Goal Driven: Are you focused on reaching a specific objective to accomplish a specific task?	1 2 3 4 5
Effective Communication: When sharing, do you follow the 4C's; clear, concise, consistent and compelling? Do you ask information seeking questions to ensure understanding?	1 2 3 4 5
Persistent: Are you determined? Do you continue to do something even when facing difficulties or opposition?	1 2 3 4 5
Personal Accountability *Do you* hold yourself accountable, take responsibility for your own actions and exercise self-control? When you make a commitment to yourself or others, do you fulfill it to the best of your abilities?	1 2 3 4 5
Results Driven: Do you strive to make things happen? Do you set specific end goals, create action plans and use tools to achieve them?	1 2 3 4 5

Total Score: _____

Add up the numbers to get a total score.

"Great leaders possess an extraordinary sense of responsibility and dedication to their fellow human beings. The qualities and characteristics of the leader will inspire others to achieve beyond their goals and meet their true potential." ~ Charmas B. Lee

OK, let us begin the journey. Over the next few chapters, I will provide you with a few more attributes and examples that, if applied, can position you with a greater chance of success. Buckle Up!

Chapter One

Communication

Perhaps one of the most essential attributes of those who have become highly successful is their ability to communicate and articulate a powerful message. If you think about some of our great leaders and the way they communicated to an individual or the masses, it is truly a thing of beauty. It has been said that the tongue is mightier than the sword. Clear, effective communication requires a strong vocabulary and an understanding of cadence, pitch, tone, and para verbals. When communication is effective, it will minimize the arc of distortion and significantly increase your chances of getting your message across. The best communicators have learned how to forge the link between attention and excellence by making what they say and how they say what they say essential and compelling.

IT'S NOT BUSINESS, IT'S PERSONAL

A counterculture thought process will be required to improve human productivity and achieve unparalleled success. Many organizations operate with a <u>bottom-line</u> *"it's not personal, it's business"* mindset. I am reminded of a scene from the romantic comedy *You've Got Mail*, starring Tom Hanks as book superstore magnate Joe Fox and Meg Ryan as independent book shop owner Kathleen Kelly. Fox is about to run Kelly out of business and suggests it's not personal.

Joe Fox: *It wasn't...personal.*

Kathleen Kelly: *What is that supposed to mean? I am so sick of that. All that means is that it's not personal to you. But it was personal to me. It's *personal* to a lot of people. And what's so wrong with being personal anyway?*

Joe Fox: *Uh, nothing.*

Kathleen Kelly: *Whatever else anything is, it ought to begin by being personal.*

Today's workforce desires a personal connection. Therefore, if the goal is to build a high-performing organization, a high-impact employee, organizational momentum, and relationship dynamics, we must recognize that Kathleen Kelly is right. ***Whatever else anything is, it ought to begin by being personal.***

Chapter Two

Advanced Personal Communication (APC)

APC requires tactical empathy, an exchange in listening. It is important to invest time in communication and unclutter the lines, both internal and external. George Bernard Shaw states, *"The single biggest problem in communication is the illusion that it has actually taken place."*

Whether the customer is looking for a product or the employee is seeking a promotion, it is about getting them to where they want to go. Your path to personal success and happiness lies in helping others arrive at their destination. In her book *Nerves of Steel*, former Southwest Airlines pilot Tammie Jo Shults provides a notable example of how to 'begin by being personal.'

Excerpt from *Nerves of Steel* – "Commercial aviation is a team sport. When a crew gathers for a flight, all crew members' names are on the paperwork, but knowing the names is not the same as meeting the people and getting to know them. *The trick is figuring out how to turn five strangers into a team in five minutes or less.* Drawing our assigned crew members together at the beginning of each day has become a habit for me, and now it is part of our protocol at Southwest Airlines. A flight crew often changes every day, sometimes multiple times throughout the day, so it takes a real effort to stop the busyness and focus for a moment on the team members. One of the best lessons I learned at home was the art of asking questions and listening attentively to the answers. It is important to me to convey that nobody needs to worry whether something is 'important enough' to tell the captain. If I take the time to look at a baby picture or listen to a personal story, the channels of communication open up. When I take the time to make my flight brief a dialogue rather than a monologue, it changes the posture of our future communications about everything, from equipment to people."

Leaders are Listeners

In Oren Harari's book titled *The Leadership Secrets of Colin Powell*, Powell states, *"The day soldiers stop bringing you their problems is the day you have stopped leading them. They have lost their confidence that you can help them or concluded that you do not care. Either case is a failure of leadership."* This statement reinforces the importance of communication and active listening.

Chapter Three

Understanding Human Behavior

With 35+ years of coaching and leadership experience, I have learned that the force multiplier in developing high-performing individuals requires an understanding of human behavior and the 10 human drives. People perform best when treated at a humanistic level. The brain, heart, mind, and soul are constructed to perform under certain conditions and dynamics. When these conditions are present, the individual will produce and thrive. **They think, behave, and perform to their capacities.**

The 10 Human Drives

These drives shape everything you think, feel, and do in life, so understanding and mastering them is critical to your success and happiness. There are 5 Baseline Drives and 5 Forward Drives. Each drive, when met, provides an inflection point to the psyche and can solicit a positive, visceral response.

The 5 Baseline Drives:	The 5 Forward Drives:
Control	Change
Competence	Challenge
Congruence	Creative Expression
Caring	Contribution
Connection	Consciousness

When you take the time to address the five baseline drives, the attitude and atmosphere of the workplace improves, which supports a climate of trust, resulting in greater productivity; here is an example of how I incorporate the 5 baseline drives into a single question: 'May I have your permission to champion you today?'

May I = Control and Caring

Your permission = Congruence and Connection

Champion you today = Competence

Ultimately, you would like your team to operate in the forward drives. This is when magic happens, creativity flows, and productivity increases. One of the reported byproducts of understanding and mastering these drives is **Discretionary Effort. Discretionary Effort** may be described as an interaction in the workplace or home where individuals give more than is expected or required from them for the benefit of the family or organization.

For more information about the 10 human drives, I would encourage you to read High Performance Coach Brendon Burchard's book *The CHARGE*, *Activating the 10 Human Drives That Make You Feel Alive.*

In the Advanced Personal Communication chapter, I introduced you to an excerpt from the book *Nerves of Steel* by former Southwestern Airlines Pilot Tammy Jo Shultz, who is able to turn 5 strangers into a team in 5 minutes or less. Captain Shultz provided us with a non-negotiable clue that great leaders possess optimism.

Chapter Four

Emotional Intelligence

H ope is the foundation of all emotional intelligence. Hope is a mental process that leads to the psychological advantages of optimism and self-confidence. People with hope have the will and strategies to achieve their goals. In the absence of hope, emotional intelligence is not sustainable. I share this with you as one of the post-pandemic realities. Many are experiencing a sense of hopelessness. They have lost their sense of self and are wrestling with debilitating discouragement.

It is showing up in every dimension of their lives, not excluding the workplace. As leaders, it is important that we recognize that almost everyone is dealing with something. Part of understanding human behavior requires us to have a high IQ in the area of emotional intelligence. Emotional Intelligence (EI) is defined as

'Someone's ability to perceive, understand and manage their own feelings and emotions' (Chignell, 2018).

Learning to regulate our emotions and mastering the skills of listening, compassion, and empathy are at a premium. Research indicates there is a direct correlation to higher job satisfaction with employees who work with or are managed by those with high EI.

The World Economic Forum ranked emotional intelligence as one of the top 10 most important workplace skills for 2020. By increasing empathy and compassion through accurate awareness and acceptance of emotions, widespread change can be ignited throughout organizations via leadership and company culture. Emotional Intelligence is a vital topic to understand by leadership at all levels.

A leader who embodies and practices high EI can:

- Communicate their vision more effectively.

- Improve their persuasion and inspirational speaking abilities.

- Ensure appropriate responses to stressful and confusing situations.

- Manage their own emotions and the emotions of their employees (to an extent).

Leadership with higher emotional intelligence has a funny way of starting a trickle-down effect of positivity and efficiency in an organization. All of this leads directly and indirectly to a more efficient, effective, and productive workplace.

There are five distinct components of EI:

1. Self-awareness

2. Self-regulation

3. Internal (or intrinsic) motivation

4. Empathy

5. Social skills

From a glance at these components, it is easy to see how higher levels of EI improve the leadership and employee connection. Leaders with higher self-regulation, intrinsic motivation, and social skills have an advantage over those with less.

Research indicates there is a direct correlation to higher job satisfaction with employees who work with or are managed by those with high EI, and it is also strongly associated with job performance. Studies have shown that organizations that invest in EI training for their employees may outperform their competitors. Researchers found that emotional intelligence training boosted employee productivity and resulted in better evaluations from management (Hosseinian et al., 2008).

- High EI (specifically high self-awareness) is negatively related to burnout and positively related to job satisfaction in people who work in the public sector (Lee, 2017).

- Nurses who had higher emotional intelligence also enjoyed higher job satisfaction (Tagoe & Quarshie, 2017).

- Teachers with higher emotional intelligence also generally perform better in their jobs (Mohamad & Jais, 2016).

- A 2017 study by Pekaar and colleagues showed that emotional intelligence significantly correlates with job performance, particularly the EI/EQ components of recognizing and managing the emotions of self and others.

- Cekmeceliogu and colleagues studied 150 call center employees and found a significant positive relationship between EI and internal job satisfaction (2012).

There are several valid, reliable, data-driven studies and resources exist on the benefits of Emotional Intelligence and its relationship to workplace performance. Below are two strategies I have read and implemented.

Emotional Intelligence at Work: The Untapped Edge for Success by Hendrie Weisinger.

How To Improve Your Emotional Intelligence at Work in Relationships by Shawn Kent Hayashi.

Chapter Five

Optimism

The leader must possess the knowledge, skills, and ability to perform their duties. Commitment, dedication, a positive attitude, and a good work ethic are the entry-level attributes of leaders who have achieved *marginal* levels of success. However, those who desire unparalleled levels of success look a little further and dig a little deeper.

Optimism is a leadership quality that will inspire others to achieve beyond their believed potential and into an area I describe as unrealized potential. Optimism is a necessary ingredient in the makeup of leadership. Great leaders make optimism an organizational priority. People become more optimistic if three **conditions** exist.

(1) They are informed and involved.

(2) They feel they have the power and authority to take action.

(3) They are committed to a compelling direction and inspiring vision.

Great leaders set the tempo and ensure these three conditions are present. This is one way the 'Great Ones' stoke the fires of optimism.

There is unmistakable evidence that people resonate with leaders who offer positive messages. I highly encourage you to read the book *Learned Optimism* by Dr. Martin Seligman. Dr. Seligman examined the presidential elections between 1900 and 1984 and concluded that American voters chose the candidates with the more optimistic message in eighteen out of twenty-two elections.

We follow a positive leader who can inspire us with hope and confidence!

- Optimism makes things happen.

- Optimism is a self-fulfilling prophecy.

- Optimism prepares the ground for inspiration.

- Optimism is a good predictor of career ascent and other things.

- Optimism spurs bold action that leads to extraordinary results.

- Optimism creates a climate of passion and enthusiasm.

Pessimism

In his book *Boundaries for Leaders: Results, Relationships, and Being Ridiculously In Charge,* Dr. Henry Cloud reminds us, *"We get what we create and what we allow."* In other words, creating an environment that yields optimum results is up to us. It is important to set boundaries around negativity and pessimism. Dean Becker, a colleague of Seligman's, shares, *"Pessimists have a way of permeating the atmosphere with dark clouds and ominous forecasts, all of which are hazardous to performance, morale, and teamwork."* Cynicism, doubt, and negativity are motivation killers. Leaders who consistently see the world through a negative lens tend to demoralize, demotivate, and undermine the effectiveness of their colleagues and employees.

Well, friends, I am of the opinion that optimism trumps pessimism every time.

Chapter Six

Connection

"Affirming people's worth and potential so clearly that they are inspired to see it in themselves." ~ Steven Covey

As a leader, it is imperative to establish rapport and trust with your employees. Only once these two components have been achieved are you able to raise expectations. Steven Covey suggests, *"Trust is the glue of life. It is the most essential ingredient in effective communication. It is the foundational principle that holds all relationships."*

Simon Sinek, author of *The Infinite Game*, has an interesting story. In chapter 6, he describes a personal experience with a barista named Noah at the coffee bar in the lobby of the Four Seasons Hotel in Las Vegas.

He states, *"It was because of Noah that I enjoyed buying that cup of coffee more than I generally enjoy."* After standing and chatting for a while, I finally asked him, *"Do you like your job?"* Without skipping a beat, Noah immediately replied, *"I love my job!"*

Based on Noah's statement, Sinek knew Noah felt an *emotional connection* to the Four Seasons that was bigger than the money he made and the job he performed. Sinek follows up with another question. *"Tell me specifically what the Four Seasons is doing that you would say you love your job?"* Noah replies, *"Throughout the day, my manager will walk past me and ask how I am doing, ask me if there is anything I need, anything they can do to help. Not just my manager...any manager. I also work for another hotel,"* he continued and shared the difference between the two hotels. At his other job, he shares that the managers walk past and try to catch people doing things wrong. Noah professes, *"I keep my head below the radar. I just want to get through the day and get my paycheck. Only at the Four Seasons,"* Noah says, *"I feel I can be myself."*

In both cases, Noah is the same person in both jobs. The only difference is the leadership environment in which he is asked to work. The leaders of the Four Seasons hotel provide us with a notable example of how the customers' experience is elevated and how the organization benefits when they invest the time to establish trust and rapport and connect with the employees. In this case, the leadership at the Four Seasons hotel prioritized their people over results, and healthy profits are a by-product of an organization that understands connection and caring. There is an old adage by Charles Swindoll in which he suggests, *"People do not care how much you know until they know how much you care."*

Chapter Seven

Contribution

"The best way to find yourself is to lose yourself in the service of others."
~ Mahatma Gandhi

There certainly was a time when the workforce and people, in general, were primarily motivated by the size of their paychecks and even perhaps making big bucks for the company they worked for, and this was reinforced through bonuses and upward mobility by their leaders. However, today's workforce shares a common trait. A powerful desire to be part of something bigger than themselves. They are much more motivated by working for a compelling purpose or cause.

Best-in-class leaders and great organizations intentionally focus on making the world a better place to live. In fact, their goods and services are designed to make consumers' lives richer, fuller, and better. Their desire for purpose, a cause, and a mission is the fuel that allows them to achieve beyond their potential and deliver unparalleled results. Purpose and meaning exist on both the organizational and individual levels.

My company, Believe and Perform like Champion's mission statement, is amazingly simple and straightforward: 'To motivate, educate and inspire others to develop a sense of greater expectations within themselves.' Consider this: each day, our team has an opportunity to create a positive change in an individual or organization's life. Our *mission* gives the team *permission* to be bold and courageous while delivering its high-impact personal and professional development services. This is a mission our team members are hungry to execute! Away from our daily workplace responsibilities and duties, you can find our local elementary or middle school team members pouring into (contributing) the lives of students who have had a challenging time in life. This contribution is 'mission-minded,' and there is a mutual benefit for the employee and the customer.

Providing value to others shifts our perspective from 'me to we,' and we focus on someone else rather than ourselves. It is mutually beneficial. A focus on what we can do to serve others is an 'outside-in' perspective. This perspective enables us to identify and solve problems for others while also creating value for ourselves. Interestingly enough, with this 'outside-in' perspective, our organization has experienced measurable increases in team cohesiveness, communication, morale, role adherence, and relational dynamics.

Chapter Eight

Coaching

According to the 2011 USADA True Sport article, *What Sport Means in America: A Survey of Sport's Role in Society*, 'Coaches are considered to be one of, if not the most, positive influences in an athlete's life.' I suggest the same applies to the workplace. The leader/coach has a tremendous influence on their employees. Coaching is essential if we want to raise our team members' performance. Sure, you can have a marginal level of success without a coach; it happens every day. People luck out or they rise to the occasion in the moment, but by winging it, they do not **grow or attain mastery**. The fastest way to get better at something is to have a coach or coaches provide you with direction. I have learned that in the absence of proper coaching, dramatic growth is impossible.

So, what is a coach?

A Coach by any other name

- Japan: sensei = one who has gone farther down the path

- Sanskrit: guru = one with great knowledge and wisdom

- Tibet: lama = one with spirituality and authority to teach

- Italy: maestro = master teacher of music

- France: tutor = private teacher

- England: guide = one who knows and shows the way

- Greece: mentor = a wise and trusted advisor

A coaching story...

For several years, I had the honor of being mentored (coached) both personally and professionally by a gentleman named Tim Devore. Tim is my kind of coach. He is brilliant, a man of God with a stunning intellect, and possesses powerful business acumen. Tim is the President of DeVore, Inc. and has worked with hundreds of CEOs, Presidents, and C-level staff to improve their productivity. While in the Air Force, Tim was a combat navigator;

now, he successfully helps others navigate their personal and professional lives. Tim has a heart of gold, however, when it comes to getting things accomplished, he is a no-nonsense kind of guy. He does not accept excuses of any kind.

I sought Tim out for some business advice. In our first coaching session, Tim asked me questions I had never thought about and was certainly not prepared to answer. He asked me about my net worth and my life plan. Tim said that to develop a blueprint for success, it would be important to know these things. By the end of the phone call, I had a list of questions I was unsure how to answer. We scheduled a follow-up call in fourteen days. Feeling overwhelmed, I hung up and walked upstairs, scratching my head. I began to second-guess my decision to ask for Tim's assistance.

My wife Janice looked at me and said, *"What is wrong, sweetheart? Are you feeling OK?" "Sweetheart,"* I replied, *"I was not equipped to answer any of Tim's questions; it is like I brought a knife to a gunfight!"* Without sk ipping a beat, she said, *"Well, what are you going to do? Now you know what it feels like to be one of your athletes when you ask them, do you want to be a champion? Of course, they do, but are they willing to do what is required of them?"* My wife is exceptionally good at offering clarity and inspiration. She has a uniqueness about her. She puts things in a context that makes sense to me. Janice will tell you she speaks 'Charmas.'

I answered Tim's questions in detail and sent them to him two days later. I guess I passed the 'Tim-test!' Over the last few years, Tim has tasked me with many things to do. He asks tough questions that can take you way out of your comfort zone. Once, in a single conversation, Tim asked me the same question three times. He really wanted me to think through my response. *"Charmas, that is not what I asked you,"* he would say, *"Please answer the question."* So, he would ask me again and again. When I finally answered the question, he would say thank you. Now, you can make an informed decision and take decisive action. Tim wanted me to be successful.

Several years ago, one of our businesses was struggling. Most of my efforts to recruit new businesses were not working, so I reached out to Tim. His advice was to change my focus, approach, and goal.

"Charmas, I want you to find a CEO whose organization is valued at a minimum of $10,000,000. Walk into their office and hand them your media kit." I was dumbfounded. I did not know anyone in those types of circles. The chorus of despair began to sing aloud in my head, asking 'fear-focused' questions. Do you have time

for this? YOU are not good enough to meet with one of those guys! Why does not Tim introduce me to one of his colleagues instead? This is going to take a lot of work, and it is probably impossible! You will not make it past the receptionist, blah, blah. After a few moments, I realized the way I viewed this **opportunity** was the problem. I was fear-focused rather than faith-focused.

I love how Theodore Roosevelt describes and offers a clarifying statement in his March 4, 1933, inaugural address. He suggests fear is *"nameless, unreasoning, unjustified terror which paralyzes needed efforts to convert retreat into advance."* On this occasion, my coach helped me recognize an obstacle: my self-limiting beliefs.

I met with a CEO whose organization was valued at $1,000,000,000. The meeting was scheduled to last 15 minutes, but instead, it lasted 45 minutes. It turned out that the CEO and I were more alike than I could have imagined and had similar philosophies about life, community, and faith.

The standards most individuals set for themselves will usually be in a comfort zone, which is well below their actual ability. If an organization is to be the best in the business, there must be a sense of greater expectations. Great leaders understand the concept of 'no pressure, no diamonds.' They know the key to finding the individual's true power lies in the psyche's deep recesses. World-class leaders use emotional drivers to motivate and inspire their people to push far beyond the norm to accomplish feats that would be impossible without this level of motivation.

The best coaches are the greatest leaders. I believe the word coach is synonymous with the word leader. In athletics, there are player-coaches. In business and life, we have leader coaches. Whether you are the parent coach, the teacher coach, the pastor coach, or the CEO coach, it does not matter.

Two of my favorite coaches who were experts at discovering their players' 'emotional drivers' were Tom Landry and Vince Lombardi.

Tom Landry

In my youth, I was afforded the opportunity to watch Coach Tom Landry about every Sunday during football season. There were many behaviors he demonstrated on a consistent basis that left a lifelong impression on me.

In a professional league led by predominately overweight coaches, *many just one cheese fry away from a major heart attack,* Coach Landry looked like he could still suit up and play.

Whether the team was winning or losing, he never got hijacked by emotion. *I interpreted this behavior to mean that, as leaders, we lose our effectiveness if we are not courteous. Just as we like to be respected, we must respect others if we want them to listen to what we say.* Coach Landry appeared to be a humble man of quiet strength and dignity.

Coach Landry was also a man of God, which is especially important to me. He was a champion both on and off the field.

Finally, he was a man who not only talked the talk but also walked the walk. If you were an athlete in the National Football League, you wanted to be coached by Tom Landry.

1972 Coach Landry led the Dallas Cowboys to Super Bowl Championship VI. I was only 11 years old. Watching his team win the Super Bowl reinforced three things for me. I wanted to become a great coach, role model, and leader of others. I wanted to develop champions and be a champion as well. Health and fitness would be important to inspire others to maintain my appearance.

I saw a documentary on ESPN about Coach Laundry's success for over 29 years. Someone asked how he could successfully forge a team out of individuals with different strengths, personalities, and abilities. Landry replied, *"My job is to get men to do what they do not want to do to achieve what they always wanted to achieve."*

Vince Lombardi

Coach Vince Lombardi took over a downtrodden Green Bay Packers team in **1959** and turned it into professional football's most dominant organization of the 1960s. Lombardi, a tireless worker with exacting standards, led Green Bay to five championships in nine seasons as head coach. His Packers won the first two Super Bowls, and the trophy given to the league champion now bears his name. Arguably, he may be the greatest professional football coach in history.

Coach Vince Lombardi was very demanding of his athletes. When they came to practice, he expected 100% of their attention. He was firm and focused. On game day, he expected his team to execute the strategies they had practiced during the week. He accepted no excuses and maintained incredibly lofty standards. His team was incredibly disciplined.

I am reminded of a speech he gave his team at their first meeting.

*"Gentlemen, we are going to pursue perfection relentlessly, knowing full well we will not catch it because nothing is perfect. However, we are going to relentlessly CHASE—IT because, in the process, we will achieve excellence. **I am not remotely interested in being just good.**"*

One of my favorite quotes from Coach Lombardi is, *"Winning becomes easy if you stick with it long enough."* Sticking with it was not about simply executing the X's and O's of the game. Coach Lombardi understood that creating and maintaining a winning **environment** was equally important as mastering the ins and outs of the game. A good leader's influence will help the team achieve its goal by outlining the requirements and coaching them to stick to the plan. The attitude of the leader affects the **atmosphere** of the workplace, and the **atmosphere** of the workplace affects other intangible factors such as employee morale, organizational momentum, and relationship dynamics. The leader's attitude, approach, and ability all tremendously affect how they can influence the desired outcome.

"In everyone's life, at some time, our inner fire goes out. It is then burst into flame by an encounter with another human being. We should all be thankful for those people who rekindle the inner flame." ~ Albert Schweitzer

My friends, you have an opportunity to be that inner flame. It is time to coach them up.

Chapter Nine

Change

*"During change, leadership is an invitation
to follow. If the leader lacks confidence, the
followers lack commitment."*

A s it relates to change, I believe Mr. Maxwell's
quote is well-stated

*"Coming together is a beginning
Keeping together is progress.
Working together is success."*
~ John Maxwell

Whenever a change is imminent, for example, in the case
of a reorganization or position change, the question on
everyone's mind is, how will this affect me? There are
4 phases of change: Precontemplation, Contemplation,

Preparation, and Action. This is the time for the leader to maintain their core values and create a compelling vision that fuels a high-octane source of energy for change.

This energy will act as a lighthouse and compass for navigating the storms that inevitably accompany the change process. We have learned that during times of uncertainty and change, most people are not looking for a hero; they are looking for a guide who gets excited every time they see them, recognizes their value, and is willing to provide them with a compass or blueprint to achieve success. Change must be wrestled with, talked through, and come to terms with. The leader must embody the mindset that success is around the corner. Be able to face the brutal facts of reality yet have an unwavering faith that not only will the organization survive, but they will also thrive and have an even greater story to tell.

People will be in various states of readiness, so change must be handled with sensitivity but also with straightforwardness. You have got to love them before you lead them. When you love your followers genuinely, they will respect and follow you through many changes. During this time, it is important that the leader:

- Maintain rapport and expressed belief in the ability to achieve a goal.

- Be honest about the *deliberate* work that is required.

- Give them a target to hit.

- Paint a vivid, 4K high-definition picture of what the sweet fragrance of success *could* be like.

- If it is possible to allow the follower to give input and be a part of the change process.

Why we are resistant to change

People who lack ownership of an idea usually resist it, even when it is in their best interest. Change tends to disrupt our routines and the habits we have created over time. Our habits do not require us to think much. First, we make our habits, and then our habits make us. Change threatens our habits and forces us to use our minds and think more. It seems silly, but our habits allow us to operate on 'automatic pilot.'

Change forces us to reevaluate and sometimes unlearn past behaviors.

When they weigh in, they buy in

People are more resistant to change when they perceive the disadvantages of change as greater than the advantages. It is important for the follower to understand what is in it for them. Leaders sometimes fail to recognize that it is human nature to weigh the advantages/disadvantages in light of personal loss/gain vs. organizational loss/gain. Change without input or power can create a sense of manipulation. There is more buy-in when we weigh in.

The 20-50-30 Rule of Change

The 20

The 20-50-30 Rule of change has been around for a long time. So, if I am dealing in generalities, the breakout usually goes like this: If there are 100 followers/employees, 20 of them are likely to be 'change friendly.' They are clear advocates who willingly embrace the change. You can depend on them to help drive the change. This group is loyal, dependable, and reliable. They tend to be your high producers. They are self-motivated and tend to work without applause. It is important not to neglect this group and devote generous attention to them during the change period. They deserve it the most, and it would be easy to take them for granted. I have learned that pouring into this group is critical, recognizing their value will reap healthy benefits down the road to change.

The 50

Again, dealing in generalities, 50 followers will be neutral. They will sit on the fence and wait and see how things progress and how others respond before they decide or not to commit. In essence, they are trying to figure out which way to lean. They are not necessarily hostile to change but are not helping like they should or could. It is important to perform a temperature check on this group. I suggest you recruit a team of 5 or so of the 20 to act as influences to move the 50 in the right direction.

The 30

The remaining 30 are the resisters. They tend to be the 'chorus of despair' antagonistic toward change and often deliberately sabotage efforts of success. When it comes to the 30, the leader must determine if the person is *unwilling or unable* to change. Willingness deals with attitude, and there is little you can do if your followers resist change because of attitude—however, the ability to change deals with perspective. Many people are willing to change, but because of the way they perceive their present circumstances and responsibilities, they refuse to do so. Joe Polish, author of *What's In It For Them,* does an excellent job of providing leaders with tools that, if applied, can affect these individuals' perspectives. Perhaps, as leaders, we need to ask ourselves a question. Is the way they see the problem (change) the problem? No matter the response, refusing to change when change is necessary is a prelude to failure. And leadership will need to make the proper decisions.

Let us look at the 4 phases and apply it to the 20-50-30 Rule.

Precontemplation: The precontemplator's resistance to change is best summarized as the four R's: reluctance, rebellion, resignation, and rationalization. This would reflect the thirty (30). This group's mind is usually already made up. In his book *Boundaries for Leaders: Results, Relationships, and Being Ridiculously In Charge,* Dr. Henry Cloud reminds us, *"We get what we create and what we allow."* In other words, it is up to the leader to create an environment that yields optimum results despite the circumstances. It is important to set boundaries around negativity and pessimism. Cynicism, doubt, and negativity are motivation killers and are contagious. It is important to set boundaries with clearly defined expectations, also called bright lines. Bright lines are unambiguous boundaries you do not cross.

Contemplation: The contemplator understands change is on the horizon and is seriously thinking about the best way to respond but has yet to make a commitment to it. This group would reflect the fifty (50). This group may simply need a little more time and more information. Simply promoting clarity will accelerate their decision-making process.

Preparation and Action: The preparer has decided to accept the change, determined the pros and cons, and committed. This reflects the twenty (20).

Understanding that nothing is more powerful than a made-up mind, they make a congruent commitment to a committed action. An invisible force gathers all around them, their energy rises, and they are major contributors to the organization. There are two major benefits to arriving at the action phase.

- Rate of skill acquisition: Defined as a decrease in time required to learn a complex motor skill resulting in efficiency, economy of effort, and self-efficacy.

- Discretionary Effort: Described as an interaction in the workplace or home where individuals give more than is required for the benefit of the organization or family.

Conflict

With change comes conflict, but conflict is growth. All of us can survive one or two moments of conflict. However, the constant battle against conflict is stressful in leadership. For example, the standards some employees set for themselves may be in a comfort zone that is well below their level. We realized there must be a sense of greater expectations, so the conflict stems from mediocrity, and the fight against mediocrity is taxing.

"Mastering the physics, politics and psychology of conflict are vital to success both personal and corporate." Sun Tzu Chinese Warrior and Philosopher. Sun Tzu wrote The Art of War 2,500 years ago, and it remains relevant today. While written as a military treatise, its guidance has also helped politicians, business leaders, and even sports teams strategically approach conflict. Dealing with conflict can be intimidating unless you understand the essentials. Sun Tzu suggests that the essentials consist of three components: Physics, Politics, and Psychology.

Physics: What am I willing to leverage in this situation?

Politics: How can I apply the 10 human drives?

Psychology: Tactical empathy is required.

I parallel conflict with the Japanese martial art form jujitsu. A colleague of mine lovingly calls negotiating conflict, verbally sparing By understanding the inherent principles of gravity, leverage, momentum, and inertia, a 95-pound woman can easily defeat a physically stronger rival. I can assure you that as a professional orator, the same applies to communication. When you are speaking, begin with the end in mind. Word selection is critical, and every sentence should be strategic. There is an inherent power that comes with sound. Speaking with passion and conviction is significant when you verbally spar; timing is everything. Another vital component is your cadence, pitch, and tone. In other words, when you are sharing information, imagine you are painting your words with a paintbrush and remember that as you speak, you create.

High-Performance Coach Brendan Burchard has a 3-part formula for thinking through any situation where conflict is present and persuasion may be necessary: mediation, negotiations, requests of your family, etc.

1. He states that our ability to acknowledge others authentically rests on the foundation. It is important to share our understanding of and appreciation for their realities explicitly. Acknowledge their challenges, struggles, and their successes before attempting to resolve the issue. I love this approach as it demonstrates empathy, creates connection, shows you care, and ultimately will create congruency, three of the 10 human drives.

2. We must also stoke their ambition for a better outcome. Doing this strengthens the connection, reinforcing our belief in them (competence). It is important to share how their actions will bring them great intrinsic rewards (personal meaning and enjoyment) as well as extrinsic rewards (social recognition, appreciation, and financial gain).

3. Finally, it is important to overlay this communication with a high dose of affect or emotion. We have to share stories or utilize our tone to help them recognize their personal value and also want to do something on an emotional level.

Here are a few more suggestions:

- Establish rules of engagement

- Begin with the end in mind

- Front-side focus (mission-minded conversations)

- Tactical empathy

- Be intentionally curious (ask information-seeking questions)

- Listen to what is not being said

- Cadence-pitch-tone and paraverbals

- Compromise on the non-essentials

- What can I do to help?

Chapter Ten

Stress and Burnout

More than 75% of all physician-related visits are for stress-related ailments and complaints. Some experts indicated that stress, anxiety, and a sense of hopelessness may be more significant contributors to these challenges than predisposed genetics, lifestyle, or nutrition. More than 120K people die per year as a direct result of work-related stress.

As leaders, stress and stress management should be a top priority for you and your employees. Excessive stress can increase the risk of high blood pressure, heart disease, and obesity over time. However, stress-related diseases also affect the gastrointestinal (GI) tract more so than any other physiological system in the body and can bring about illnesses and conditions such as ulcers, acid reflux, colitis, irritable bowel syndrome, and Chron's disease.

Paying attention to the important link between stress and nutrition is imperative.

- Stress affects all aspects of human nutrition.

- Bodies are not going to digest food or absorb nutrients properly.

- Metabolisms will suffer (extreme weight gain or loss).

- Certain foods trigger the body's stress response, resulting in serious health consequences.

The good news is that the reverse holds true—by choosing certain foods, changing eating habits, and making more conscientious nutritional decisions, we can reduce stress and even reverse its harmful effects on the body.

Signs of Burnout

It is important to recognize the physical and behavioral symptoms of burnout.

Physical

- Fatigue & physical exhaustion

- Headaches & GI disturbances

- Weight loss

- Sleeplessness

- Depression

- Shortness of breath

Behavioral

- Changeable mood

- Increased irritability

- Loss of caring for people

- Lowered tolerance or frustration

- Suspiciousness of others

- Feelings of helplessness

- Lack of control

- Greater professional risk-taking

Burnout occurs in three stages: the stress arousal stage, the energy conservation stage and the exhaustion stage. Burnout progresses from Stage 1 through Stage 3, although the process can be interrupted and reversed at any time. Girdano, Everly, & Dusek (1993, p. 57) have developed a self-evaluative checklist that describes the symptoms and behavior exhibited in each stage. It is advisable to review this checklist periodically.

Stage 1: The Stress Arousal Stage (includes any two of the following symptoms)

- Persistent irritability

- Persistent anxiety

- Period of high blood pressure

- Bruxism (grinding your teeth at night)

- Insomnia

- Forgetfulness

- Heart palpitations

- Unusual heart rhythms

- Inability to concentrate

- Headaches

Stage 2: The Energy Conservation Stage (includes any two of the following symptoms)

- Lateness for work

- Procrastination

- Need 3-day weekends

- Decreased sexual desire

- Persistent tiredness in the mornings

- Turning work in late

- Social withdrawal

- Cynical attitudes

- Resentfulness

- Increased alcohol consumption

- Increased coffee, tea, or cola consumption

Stage 3: The Exhaustion Stage (includes any two of the following symptoms)

- Chronic sadness or depression

- Chronic stomach or bowel problems

- Chronic mental fatigue

- Chronic physical fatigue

- Chronic headaches

- Desire to 'drop out' of society

- Perhaps the desire to commit suicide

However, Girdano, Everly & Dusek (1993) emphasize that "burnout is not permanent—it is reversible; furthermore, it is preventable. RELAXATION, PROPER DIET, and PHYSICAL EXERCISE help you recover from burnout and prevent this problem from ever occurring."

References

Burchard, B. (2012) *The CHARGE, Activating the 10 Human Drives That Make You Feel Alive*: Free Press Simon & Schuster

Cloud, H. (2013) *Boundaries for Leaders, Results Relationships and Being Ridiculously in Charge*: New York, Harper Collins

Covey, S. (1989) *The 7 Habits of Highly Effective People, Powerful Lessons in Personal Change:* New York, Free Press

Drive Leadership Group, (2024) *Why Employees are Really Quitting:* dlg.org

Harari, O. (2002) *The Leadership Secrets of Colin Powell*: McGraw Hill

Harkavy, D. (2007) *Becoming a Coaching Leader, The proven Strategy for Building a Team of Champions*: Thomas Nelson Publishers

Harvard Business Review in Conjunction with Tony Schwarts

How to Improve Emotional Intelligence: (2013) Positive Psychology.com

Lee, C. (2018) *Stay in Your Lane, The best leaders are the greatest coaches*: Live the Epic Life

Lencioni, P. (2000) *The Four Obsessions of an Extraordinary Executive, A Leadership Fable*: Jossey-Bass

Remember the Titans, (2010) *Attitude Reflects Leadership*

Shults, T. (2019) *Nerves of Steel, How I followed my dreams earned my wings and faced my greatest challenge*: W Publishing Group

Sinek S. (2019) *The Infinite Game*: Penguin Random House

Vernacchia, R., McGuire, R. & Cook, D. (1996) *Coaching mental excellence, It does matter whether you win or lose...:* Portola Valley CA, Warde Publishers

You've Got Mail (1998)

Acknowledgements

As entrepreneurs, we have learned that when an individual pushes his or her limits, they quickly find them, but when a team pushes its limits, it can move the earth. We would like to recognize all those individuals who contributed to this project, from the publishing experts and our graphic designer to all those individuals who took time to read this manuscript and provide the foreword, testimonials, and constructive feedback.

Time is the most precious commodity that we have. Thank you for investing your time in the project.

Military Might Publishing

Trevor Nolan

Joanne Stewart

Geraldine Villanueva

Dr. Clarence Shuler

Dr. MelindaJoy Mingo

Russ Council

Bryan Aspenson

Frank Sinclair

Chip Frazer

Joe Aldaz

Ramon Alvarez

Jamey Ciesielski

About the Authors

Charmas and Janice Lee are the co-owners of Believe and Perform like Champions, a business specializing in improving human productivity, located in Colorado Springs, CO. For more than 21 years, Mr. and Mrs. Lee have been challenging individuals to transform their lives through their dynamic brand of facilitated introspection, motivation, and personal development. They have worked successfully with thousands of individuals in the academic, athletic, and business arenas using mindset coaching...a high-performance mental mastery model that suggests life is 5% psychological and 95% physiological. However, the 5 controls the 95. Their unique approach to lifelong positive change is cultivated from extensive professional experience building champion athletes who have competed at various levels of competition, including the National Football League, United States Figure Skating Association, World Boxing Organization, and USA Track and Field. These insights have been adapted into comprehensive strategies that improve human productivity and will help you achieve unparalleled levels of success. Together, they have published 6 books currently available on Amazon.com and CharmasLee.com.

Charmas and Janice live in Colorado Springs, CO. Together, they are known as the perfect team and answer to the name "**Team Lee.**' It has been rumored that the only things they cannot do are perform surgery and fly helicopters.

To learn more, please visit CharmasLee.com.